# GREAT INVENTIONS

# THE TELESCOPE AND MICROSCOPE

By Robin Doak

**WORLD ALMANAC® LIBRARY**

Please visit our web site at: www.worldalmanaclibrary.com
For a free color catalog describing World Almanac® Library's list of high-quality books and multimedia programs, call 1-800-848-2928 (USA) or 1-800-387-3178 (Canada). World Almanac® Library's fax: (414) 332-3567.

Library of Congress Cataloging-in-Publication Data

Doak, Robin S. (Robin Santos), 1963-
     The telescope and microscope / by Robin Doak.
        p. cm. — (Great inventions)
     Includes bibliographical references and index.
     ISBN 0-8368-5880-8 (lib. bdg.)
     ISBN 0-8368-6592-8 (softcover)
     1. Optical instruments—Juvenile literature.  2. Telescopes—Juvenile literature.  3. Microscopes—Juvenile literature.
     I. Title.  II.  Great inventions (Milwaukee, Wis.)
     QC371.4.D63   2005
     681'.41—dc22                                            2005041615

First published in 2006 by
**World Almanac® Library**
A Member of the WRC Media Family of Companies
330 West Olive Street, Suite 100
Milwaukee, WI  53212  USA

A Creative Media Applications, Inc. Production
Design and Production: Alan Barnett, Inc.
Editor: Susan Madoff
Copy Editor: Laurie Lieb
Proofreaders: Tania Bissell, Laurie Lieb
Indexer: Nara Wood
World Almanac® Library editor: Carol Ryback
World Almanac® Library art direction: Tammy West
World Almanac® Library production: Jessica Morris

Photo credits: © Stapleton Collection/CORBIS: page 4; Photo.com: pages 5, 17, 29; © The Granger Collection: pages 8, 13, 31, 32, 34; © AP/Wide World Photos: pages 7, 9, 14, 18, 22, 24, 25, 26, 27, 38, 39, 41; diagrams by Rolin Graphics.

Printed in the United States of America

1 2 3 4 5 6 7 8 9 09 08 07 06 05

# TABLE OF CONTENTS

**CHAPTER 1**  A Scientific Revolution . . . . . . . . . . . . . . . . . 4

**CHAPTER 2**  Seeing a New Universe . . . . . . . . . . . . . . 9

**CHAPTER 3**  Many Ways of Seeing Stars . . . . . . . . . . 17

**CHAPTER 4**  Peering into the Future . . . . . . . . . . . . . 25

**CHAPTER 5**  Looking at Tiny Life . . . . . . . . . . . . . . . . 29

**CHAPTER 6**  Types of Microscopes . . . . . . . . . . . . . . 36

**CHAPTER 7**  Microscopes Today . . . . . . . . . . . . . . . . 39

Time Line . . . . . . . . . . . . . . . . . . . . . . 44

Glossary . . . . . . . . . . . . . . . . . . . . . 45

For More Information . . . . . . . . . . . . . . . 46

Index . . . . . . . . . . . . . . . . . . . . . . . . . 47

Words that appear in the glossary are printed in
**boldface** type the first time they appear in the text.

# 1 A SCIENTIFIC REVOLUTION

For most of history, human understanding of the world was limited to what people could see with their unaided eyes. Objects that were far away were not easy to understand, nor were things that were very small, such as germs. Even some objects and events that could be seen, such as meteor showers, the phases of the moon, and epidemics of disease, were impossible to understand and explain.

In an attempt to create a logical world where everything made sense, ancient philosophers created theories about scientific mysteries. In ancient China, for example, people believed that a solar eclipse was caused by a dragon swallowing the Sun. Disease and

▼ Ancient astrologers used different instruments to study the night sky. (Print by Ambrosius Macrobius).

sickness were thought to be the judgment of an angry god against a sinful person. As time went on, early scientists, physicians, and astronomers (people who study stars and other objects in space) began searching for better explanations.

## A Time for Science

For many centuries, the theories set out by the ancient philosophers were accepted as fact: Until the late 1500s, there was no possible way to prove the ancient ideas correct or incorrect. The move toward a better understanding of the universe began during the Renaissance (the fourteenth through the sixteenth centuries).

The Renaissance was a time of great artistic and intellectual freedom and scientific advancement. Scholars and philosophers became intensely interested in exploring the world around them. As a result, they perfected the scientific method. The scientific method is a system of research that begins with a question about nature. Scholars answer the question after careful testing and research. During this period, the printing press proved one of the most important inventions. With the introduction of movable type, printers produced books and pamphlets in mass quantities. Knowledge became easier to share, and scholars gained more access to the work of those who had gone before.

The telescope and the microscope are both examples of the Renaissance quest for answers. Telescopes make distant objects seem closer and larger. Microscopes make tiny objects seem larger. Both inventions allow humans to take a closer, clearer look at their world.

▲ *This early refracting telescope sits on a base that allows it to swivel in all directions.*

## Through a Lens

The history of both the telescope and the microscope begins with one simple item: the glass lens. The ancient Egyptians were the first people to make glass. More than five thousand years ago, they created glass from silica, a hard, white or colorless substance, and natron, a natural, saltlike substance.

About two thousand years ago, people may have looked through water-filled globes to magnify small items. Ancient Greeks wrote about devices known as burning glasses: pieces of glass used to burn holes in documents to "erase" certain parts of text.

These early glasses were **convex**—fatter in the middle than at the edges. They were fitted into a frame so people could see small objects more clearly. Because the glass pieces were shaped like lentils, they became known as lenses, from the Latin word for "lentil."

Some historians credit an Italian monk named Alexandro della Spina with inventing the first pair of eyeglasses, sometime between 1285 and 1300.

## Stonehenge: An Early Observatory?

Many centuries ago, prehistoric people set up huge gray blocks of stone to form circles in the middle of a field in the English countryside, 90 miles (144 kilometers) west of London. The oldest parts of the gigantic monument may date to about 2800 B.C. For centuries, people have wondered who placed the stones there and why.

Some archaeologists believe that the site was an ancient observatory, a place where prehistoric people examined the night sky. These ancient people may have used the stones to help them chart certain astronomical events, such as the summer solstice (the longest day of the year) and the winter solstice (the shortest day of the year). Some scientists suggest that the monument was used to predict lunar eclipses.

Eyeglasses and magnifying lenses later became popular with elderly scholars whose eyesight was failing.

Despite the invention of these new tools, human understanding of the universe and other areas of science remained limited and faulty. Then, in the early 1600s, the invention of the telescope opened up new worlds of exploration.

## Seeking Answers in the Stars

Humans began carefully observing and documenting the night skies centuries ago. Ptolemy (c. 100–165), was one of the first people to create a map of the heavens. Ptolemy, an Egyptian of Greek descent, organized the stars visible from the Northern Hemisphere into forty-eight **constellations,** or groupings. Ancient Chinese and Arab astronomers also studied the arrangements of the stars. (We offically recognize eighty-eight constellations today.)

Early astronomers developed crude instruments, such as the *merkhet,* used in Egypt, to advance their quest for knowledge. The merkhet, the "instrument of knowing," was a notched stick with which the Egyptians measured the positions and movements of stars and planets. They also used the merkhet to align the pyramids squarely in each direction.

The ancient Greeks invented a device called an **astrolabe.** An astrolabe is a metal disk with a round frame that measures the altitude, or height, of stars

▲ *Stonehenge is possibly an ancient observatory that may date back to 2800* B.C. *Archaeologists theorize that it was built in three phases over hundreds of years and that transporting and erecting the stones required approximately thirty million hours of labor. The remaining stones average 18 feet (5.5 meters) in height and weigh 25 tons (22.5 tonnes) each. Mystery still surrounds this ancient monument. The ruins of Stonehenge and its remarkable engineering have inspired many theories about the culture of an ancient civilization.*

and planets above the horizon. Later, Ptolemy developed an instrument called a **quadrant**. A quadrant was shaped like a quarter circle with a scale that marked out ninety degrees. Like the astrolabe, it measures the altitude of a star or planet.

French Jewish scholar Levi ben Gershon developed the cross-staff in the early 1300s. This device was a long, wooden stick with a movable crosspiece. It measured the angle between two stars.

## Explaining Illness

At the same time early astronomers were seeking to understand the stars, people were also trying to explain sickness and disease. Greek physicians, such as Hippocrates and Galen, for example, believed that people became ill when the body's humors, or liquids, were not in balance. As time went on, people realized that some diseases could spread from one person to another. The invention of the microscope gave scientists the tool to study and learn about the germs and viruses that spread diseases.

## Present-Day Science

Imagine the modern world without telescopes and microscopes. Without telescopes, human knowledge about Earth's place in the universe would be restricted to what is visible with the naked eye.

Likewise, without microscopes, people would know far less about biology, chemistry, and many other sciences. Humans would have no idea how energy is produced or what happens when chemicals interact.

Indeed, without the invention of the telescope and the microscope, the history of the world for the last four hundred years would be very different.

▲ *An etching of Hippocrates (c. 460–377 B.C.), a Greek physician and scientist who put forth early theories about the human body and disease in approximately 460 B.C.*

*The Telescope and Microscope*

# SEEING A NEW UNIVERSE

In the late 1200s, people began making spectacles that made small objects seem larger. In 1608, a Dutch optician named Hans Lippershey invented a "spyglass" by placing two glass lenses inside a narrow tube.

News of the invention soon spread to other European nations. In Italy, scientist Galileo Galilei learned of the spyglass. In 1609, he used what he had been told about the spyglass to create a tool to view the stars and planets. Galileo used his instrument to make small objects on Earth look larger.

Galileo's device was a **refracting telescope**. Refracting telescopes work by focusing light rays and directing them to an eyepiece. Light rays enter the telescope's body and pass through a lens, called the objective lens. The rays are bent (refracted) toward a focal point at the other end of the tube. After the rays meet at the focus, they they pass through the eyepiece, which is a second lens (also called an ocular lens). The image appears inverted: everything is upside-down and backward.

Galileo's first telescope magnified items to three or four times their normal size. His later telescopes were

▼ Galileo Galilei's quest for knowledge of the universe led to the invention of the refracting telescope.

## A Sun-Centered Universe

More than sixty-five years before Galileo began exploring the skies with his telescopes, Polish astronomer Nicolaus Copernicus (1473–1543) put forth a radical new vision of outer space. Most scholars of the time accepted that the Sun and planets revolved around Earth, which was considered the center of the universe. Copernicus believed, however, that Earth and all the planets revolved around the Sun. Although Copernicus's theory seemed logical to some people, the Catholic Church considered it dangerous. Catholic authorities believed that the theory contradicted the Bible, and they did not want anyone questioning the Bible. Without the proper tools, Copernicus had no way of proving his theory right or wrong. Today, Copernicus is known as the "father of modern astronomy."

## Fast Fact

Viewers looking through early refracting telescopes saw a rainbow of colors around the edge of the image. The shape of the convex lens changes the speed of the light rays passing through it, which separates the light into different wavelengths and causes this colorful artifact.

even more powerful. Within a year, Galileo had built a telescope that was thirty times more powerful than the human eye. At this time, however, the only way to create a more powerful telescope was to make its tube larger and use bigger lenses.

The telescope revolutionized the way people thought about the universe and their place in it. In December 1609, Galileo turned his telescope to the sky and studied the Moon. Even though his first glimpses of the Moon were fuzzy and inverted, Galileo saw that the surface of the Moon was not smooth, as Aristotle had claimed; instead, it was dotted with craters and mountains, just like Earth.

New discoveries followed. Galileo saw Jupiter's moons and hundreds of previously unknown stars in the Milky Way Galaxy through his telescope. In the coming years, as telescopes became more powerful, astronomers learned more about space. Their new knowledge led to a better understanding of Earth.

*The Telescope and Microscope*

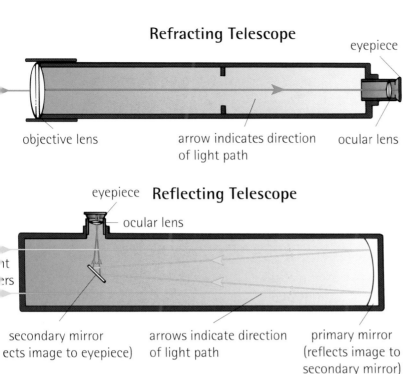

## Refracting Telescope

eyepiece

objective lens

arrow indicates direction
of light path

ocular lens

## Reflecting Telescope

eyepiece

ocular lens

secondary mirror
(reflects image to eyepiece)

arrows indicate direction
of light path

primary mirror
(reflects image to
secondary mirror)

*◀ A refracting tele-scope uses a system of lenses to magnify an object. The objective lens collects light and focuses it on a second lens, the eyepiece, which brings the image into focus for the viewer.*

*A reflecting telescope uses curved mirrors to collect and focus light. Light enters the optical tube and reflects off a concave mirror at the other end, which reflects the image to a second mirror and into the eyepiece. Reflecting telescopes can be made larger than refracting telescopes because it is easier to produce mirrored lenses with a larger diameter than large-diameter glass lenses. Also, large glass lenses used in refrac-tors become too heavy for practical use in tel-escopes and can distort under their own weight.*

# Reflecting Telescopes

Although the invention of the telescope was a milestone in science, the instrument itself had serious limitations. Because the only way to make telescopes more power-ful was to make them larger, the strongest instruments were huge, awkward devices. One of the largest refracting telescopes was built by Polish astronomer Johannes Hevelius about 1673. The supersized scope was 150 feet (46 meters) long and extremely difficult to operate. As a result, it was rarely used.

Scientists soon began searching for ways to build telescopes that did not need to be bigger to be better. In 1668, English scientist Isaac Newton (1642–1727) solved the problem. Newton developed the first working **reflecting telescope**. The reflecting telescope works by gathering, focusing, and magnifying light rays emitted by an object.

Unlike Galileo's refracting telescope, Newton's device did not include a lens at the front. Instead, he placed a **concave** (curving inward) mirror at the back of the tube. The bowl-shaped mirror reflected light rays back onto a second flat mirror that was placed below an eyepiece. Newton's eyepiece was located in the side of the tube toward the front of the telescope.

In the 1600s, glass grinders were unable to create a mirror capable of being used inside a telescope. To make the new device work, Newton had to build his own mirror. So he created a tiny, one-inch (2.54-centimeter) surface out of copper, tin, and arsenic, a semimetallic element. Newton carefully polished the concave surface, making it shiny enough to reflect light rays effectively.

In 1672, Newton presented his new telescope to the world. Scientists were thrilled: The study of the sky could continue in ways not possible before. Over the years, other scientists improved the reflecting telescope. Each improvement allowed people to see into space more clearly than ever before.

## Telescope Improvements

In many ways, the reflecting telescope was an improvement over the refracting telescope, but it was not perfect. For example, images still appeared upside down.

In 1672, the same year Newton shared his invention with the world, a Frenchman named Cassegrain had designed his own reflecting telescope. Cassegrain's device included a hole in the primary, concave mirror. The hole focused light rays onto a secondary, convex mirror, which in turn reflected the rays back through the hole and into the eyepiece. Images seen through Cassegrain's telescopes were much less blurry than through Newton's telescopes.

In the early 1700s, scientists continued to improve the quality of mirrors used in reflecting telescopes.

Using the human eye as their model, they were able to produce mirrors with a parabaloid, or cone-shaped, surface. Improvements in the mirrors resulted in clearer images.

German-born scientist Sir William Herschel (1738–1822) worked hard to advance the science of astronomy. As a young man living in England, Herschel became interested in building reflecting telescopes that would allow him to see as far as the outer limits of the universe. In the late 1700s, Herschel built a number of devices, including the largest usable telescope ever built. His telescope was 40 feet (12 m) long and used a 2,000-pound (908-kilogram) mirror that measured 4 feet (1.2 m) in diameter.

From his observatory in Slough, England, Herschel pointed telescopes at the sky. During a career that spanned more than fifty years, he made many important astronomical discoveries. In 1781, for example, he spotted the planet Uranus. He called the planet *Georgium sidus,* or George's star, for King George III of Great Britain. (It was later renamed by German astrologer Johann Bode, and by 1827 was commonly known as Uranus.) Herschel also studied the movements of the Sun and created the first theories of how stars were formed. Today, a telescope named for Herschel operates on the Canary Islands in the Atlantic Ocean off the west coast of Africa.

▼ *An engraving of what was in 1700 the world's largest telescope, used by the German-born astronomer Sir William Herschel. Herschel discovered the planet Uranus with this instrument.*

# Catadioptric Telescopes

In 1930, an Estonian optician named Bernhard Schmidt (1879–1935) developed a telescope that combined elements of both the refracting and reflecting telescopes. The instrument was named the catadioptric telescope, but it is sometimes called the refracting-reflecting telescope. Schmidt's device combined the refracting telescope's front lens with the reflecting telescope's mirror at the back.

The lens of the catadioptric telescope was specially designed to bend light rays and correct the blurriness of the scope's image. As a result, the lens is known as the **corrector lens**. Thanks to Schmidt's invention, astronomers were now able to see larger areas of the sky at one time.

Today, there are two different types of catadioptric telescopes: the Schmidt-Cassegrain telescope and the Maksutov-Cassegrain telescope. The telescopes use different types of corrector lenses.

▶ *A picture of Venus (dot, bottom right) in transit across the face of the Sun in June 2004, as seen from a Schmidt-Cassegrain telescope. The image was taken by a digital camera attached to the 8-inch (20-cm) telescope.*

# Big Twentieth-Century Scopes

At the turn of the twentieth century, scientists in the United States began building some of the biggest and best telescopes in the world. In 1897, for example, the world's largest refracting telescope went into operation at the Yerkes Observatory in Williams Bay, Wisconsin. This telescope, which features a 40-inch (102-cm) lens of polished glass, is still the largest refractor in the world. Run by the University of Chicago, it is still used for astronomical research.

In 1908, George Elliot Hale built a reflecting telescope with a 60-inch (152-cm) mirror on Mount Wilson near Pasadena, California. The largest telescope in the world at that time, it was used by astronomers to study sunspots and solar radiation and to create a system for classifying stars. Although it is no longer used for scientific research, visitors to the Mount Wilson Observatory can still peek into the sky through the huge device.

In 1917, scientists began constructing an even bigger telescope at the Mount Wilson Observatory. With a 100-inch (254-cm) mirror, the new scope was much more powerful than other telescopes. It was named the Hooker telescope for John D. Hooker, the man who helped pay for the gigantic mirror.

In the years to come, the Hooker telescope revealed the answers to many mysteries. From 1919 to 1924, for example, Edwin Hubble used it to prove that other galaxies besides the Milky Way existed in space. The discovery was a major milestone in human understanding of the size of the universe. Hubble later used the Hooker to show that the limits of the universe were constantly expanding. This discovery would lead scientists to develop the "Big Bang" theory of the universe. According to this theory, the universe was formed by a huge, hot explosion that

## The Hooker Telescope

- The Hooker telescope mirror weighs nearly 900 pounds (409 kg). Cast in St. Gobain, France, in 1908, it is still the largest solid glass mirror ever manufactured.

- When the big mirror was cast, sheets of bubbles formed between the mirror's layers. Some glass experts believe that the bubbles actually help the mirror work more accurately when changing temperatures place stresses on the glass.

- The telescope tube measures 11 feet (3.4 m) in diameter. The tube, mirror, and other moving parts weigh about 100 tons (91 tonnes).

- Beginning in 1919, physicist Albert Michelson used the telescope to measure the speed of light.

- The Hooker telescope was the largest in the world until 1948. That year, a telescope with a 200-inch (5-meter) mirror was built on Palomar Mountain near Pasadena, California.

# Making a Simple Telescope

All you need to make a functional refracting telescope are two lenses. Here's how to do it.

**Here's What You Need:**

**An objective lens:** Find a large, weak convex lens (thinner at the edges than in the center; use a magnifying glass or check out your nearest hobby shop)

**An eyepiece:** Find a small but powerful concave lens (thinner in the center than at the edges; look for a photographer's loupe, ask an optician for an old lens, or check out your nearest hobby shop)

**Here's What to Do:**

1. Choose an object to focus on in the distance.
2. With one hand, hold the large lens out in front of you.
3. With the other hand, hold the small lens up to your eye.
4. Adjust the distance between the two lenses until you get a clear view of your object.

You've made a working telescope! To make your scope more permanent, use a cardboard tube to create a body. Attach a lens at either end, and see what happens!

took place between ten billion and twenty billion years ago. Astronomers also used the Hooker telescope to find ways to calculate distances from Earth to the stars.

As telescopes became larger and more powerful, they not only helped scientists answer many questions but also raised new ones. For example, scientists wanted to learn more about the age and size of the universe. They wanted to understand more about how stars and planets form. Astronomers soon realized, however, that the only way to find the answers to these questions was somehow to place a telescope in space, beyond the distorting effects of Earth's atmosphere (the mass of gases that surround the planet). For many decades, this feat remained impossible.

# 3 MANY WAYS OF SEEING STARS

Telescopes come in many different sizes. Some telescopes are small. Binoculars, for example, are two side-by-side, portable telescopes that can be carried just about anywhere. Other telescopes are gigantic.

Despite their differences, all telescopes have certain elements in common. The most important thing about all telescopes, of course, is that these instruments allow humans to see and learn about objects that are outside the normal field of vision. Scientists use certain terms to describe these instruments.

▲ *Binoculars, like this old model, essentially contain two telescopes mounted side-by-side and small enough to carry around. Beginning observers find binoculars a useful tool for learning the sky.*

## Talking about Optical Telescopes

Refracting and reflecting telescopes are called **optical telescopes**. Like the human eye, optical telescopes work with visible light rays.

The main lens of an optical telescope is the objective lens, or the objective. The diameter of the objective or mirror is its **aperture**. The larger a telescope's aperture, the more light it gathers and the clearer the images it produces.

▲ *Caught between night and day, Halley's comet streaks through the sky in this image from January 1986. A charge-coupled device on a 16-inch (40-cm) telescope at the National Astronomy Observatories in Cerro Tolodo, Chile, captured the image.*

Large telescopes must be placed on some sort of movable structure, called a mount. Part of the mount, known as the yoke, holds the telescope's center. The yoke rotates on a circular support, allowing the telescope to follow an object as it moves across the sky.

Today, few professional astronomers look through the eyepieces of optical telescopes. Instead, they use a **charge-coupled device**, or CCD. Just like your digital camera, the CCD is an electronic sensor that takes digital pictures of the sky. Astronomers set the CCD to track and record objects moving across the sky. They can then view the pictures at any time—without staying up all night.

Optical telescopes allow astronomers to see visible light rays, but as scientists learned more about light and the universe, they discovered that some rays in space are invisible to the human eye. Such light includes **infrared radiation**, ultraviolet radiation, radio waves, and X-rays. To learn more about certain objects in the sky, scientists had to find a way to study these invisible rays.

## Radio Telescopes

One type of telescope used to detect invisible light rays is the radio telescope. A radio telescope is used to detect and record radio waves that are emitted by planets, stars, and other objects in space.

Radio telescope differ from optical telescopes. Instead of lenses and mirrors, a radio telescope uses a large receiver called a "dish" to detect radio waves. These waves are translated into electrical signals and analyzed by a computer. The computer creates an image of the object in space using the electrical signals.

One of the first radio telescopes was built in New Jersey in the early 1930s. In 1932, scientist Karl Guthe Jansky (1905–1950) created a device capable of detecting radio waves emitted by stars in the Milky Way. Over the years, more powerful radio telescopes have enabled scientists to collect radio waves from even deeper space. Radio telescopes helped astronomers detect space gases and pulsars. Pulsars are rapidly spinning stars that give off strong beams of radio waves.

The largest radio telescope in the world is located near Arecibo in Puerto Rico. The Arecibo Radio Telescope has a dish that measures 1,000 feet (305 m) in diameter. Built in 1963, the telescope is used not only to record radio waves but also to send them into outer space. In 1974, for example, a group of scientists sent a radio message into deep space in the hopes of contacting extraterrestrial life. So far, no signals have been received in return.

Another important radio telescope observatory is the Very Large Array (VLA) near Socorro, New Mexico. The VLA is made up of twenty-seven movable radio dishes that work together to give astronomers an expanded view of the sky. Another group of radio telescopes is the Very Large Baseline Array (VLBA). The ten supersensitive telescopes are spread across the United States from New Hampshire to Hawaii. Data from the telescopes are analyzed in Socorro, New Mexico.

## Infrared Telescopes

Infrared radiation was one of the first invisible rays discovered. The **wavelength** of infrared radiation is longer than that of visible light rays. (A wavelength is the distance between the peak of one wave of light

### Jocelyn Bell Burnell, Pulsar Detective

Jocelyn Bell Burnell was born in Belfast, Ireland, in 1943. She developed her interest in astronomy at a young age. Later, as a graduate student at Cambridge University in England, she helped build a huge radio telescope. The telescope began working in 1967. Burnell's job was to operate the enormous instrument and analyze the charts of the universe that it created.

While studying the charts, Burnell noticed something out of the ordinary. In fact, the object was like nothing that had ever been seen before. Burnell had become the first person to discover a pulsar, or a rapidly spinning star. Since the 1930s, astronomers had suspected that such stars existed. Until Burnell's discovery, however, no one had been able to prove it.

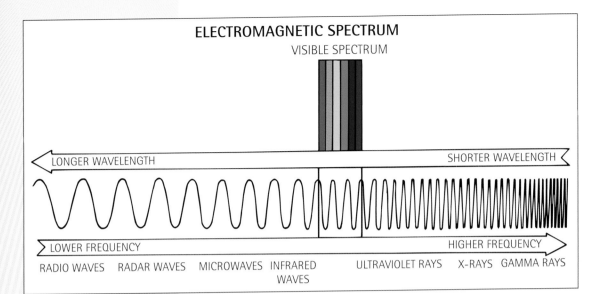

ELECTROMAGNETIC SPECTRUM
VISIBLE SPECTRUM

LONGER WAVELENGTH    SHORTER WAVELENGTH

LOWER FREQUENCY    HIGHER FREQUENCY

RADIO WAVES    RADAR WAVES    MICROWAVES    INFRARED WAVES    ULTRAVIOLET RAYS    X-RAYS    GAMMA RAYS

▲ *Planetary bodies radiate electromagnetic energy of varying frequency and wavelengths. Frequency is the number of waves that pass through a point in space during a timed interval. The electromagnetic spectrum is broken up into specific regions.*

*The visible light spectrum falls in a narrow region. Individual wavelength within the visible light region represent a particular color.*

*The amount of energy in a light wave is related to its frequency. Gamma rays have a high frequency and the most energy. Low frequency radio waves have the least energy.*

and the peak of the next wave.) Humans experience infrared radiation as heat.

Sir William Herschel discovered infrared radiation in 1800. In the 1920s, American physicist William Weber Coblentz (1873–1962) built a device to measure the infrared radiation of stars. Today's infrared telescopes are usually reflecting telescopes with a special electronic device attached. The device, which takes the place of the CCD on a regular reflecting telescope, is called an **infrared array detector.**

Because an infrared telescope is built to detect heat, certain parts of the instrument must always be kept cold. Exposure to any sort of warmth could interfere with readings from space. In addition, these telescopes must be used at high altitudes. Some high-flying research aircraft carry infrared telescopes. The Kuiper Airborne Observatory (KAO), for example, uses an infrared telescope. The KAO, a converted cargo plane, is the only airborne observatory in the world. Its pilots fly high above the clouds and take telescopic images of space. Astronomers on the flying observatory were the first to discover the nine thin rings of Uranus.

Other infrared telescopes are placed in satellites and launched into space. One such scope was the Infrared Astronomy Satellite (IRAS). Launched in 1983, IRAS's mission was to map the entire sky in infrared wavelengths. It completed its mission in just ten months. IRAS was the first space telescope to discover a comet. It also discovered a new type of galaxy called a starburst galaxy, where new stars form more quickly than in other galaxies.

## Ultraviolet Radiation

German scientist Johann Wilhelm Ritter (1776–1810) discovered ultraviolet rays in 1801. Ultraviolet rays have very short wavelengths. They are also called UV rays. Overexposure to UV rays causes sunburn and skin cancer in humans.

Scientists soon realized that reflecting telescopes set up on Earth could capture pictures of most

## Keck Observatory

A dormant volcano in Hawaii is home to some supersized telescopes. Keck Observatory, on the summit of Mauna Kea, on the Island of Hawaii is home to the world's largest optical and infrared telescopes. Each enormous telescope stands eight stories tall and weighs 300 tons (272 tonnes). The observatory's optical telescope 's mirror is made up of thirty-six different parts. The mirror measures 400 inches (1,016 cm) in diameter—more than 33 feet (10 m) across!

Keck Observatory began operating in 1993. Since then, astronomers using these telescopes have made some amazing discoveries. They discovered black holes in the center of a galaxy forty million light-years from Earth. The Keck telescopes also helped the scientist calculate how fast the universe is expanding.

ultraviolet rays. Some of the shortest ultraviolet wavelengths, however, called **extreme ultraviolet rays** were not detectable. New technology was needed.

In the last quarter of the twentieth century, highly sensitive telescopes were constructed to detect the shortest UV rays. One such scope, the International Ultraviolet Explorer (IUE), was launched into space in 1978. The telescope, in use until 1996, provided scientists with new information about the universe. They collected data about galaxies, black holes, solar winds, and much more.

Another important ultraviolet telescope is the Hopkins Ultraviolet Telescope (HUT). HUT, which is used only in space, detects even the shortest UV rays. HUT was used for a total of forty hours during two space shuttle missions. In that short time, the telescope provided information that helped astronomers better understand the makeup of distant galaxies, black holes, and supernovas (stars that explode and

► In October 2003, astronomers at the Keck Observatory in Waimea, Hawaii, discovered the Lynx Arc megastar cluster. The cluster is the biggest, brightest, and hottest yet discovered in the universe.

*The Telescope and Microscope*

become much brighter than regular stars). Because of limited NASA funding and the discontinuation of shuttle flights, there are currently no plans to use HUT again. Visitors to the Air and Space Museum in Washington, D.C., can see the telescope there.

# X-Ray and Gamma Ray Telescopes

Many objects in space—black holes, supernovas, the Sun, other stars, and some comets—emit X-rays and gamma rays, which cannot penetrate Earth's atmosphere. Astronomers need a way to observe these rays to learn more about them. Scientists built special telescopes to detect X-rays and gamma rays, the electromagnetic radiation with the shortest wavelengths.

Unlike regular light rays, X-rays are absorbed—not reflected—by mirrors. Some X-ray telescopes use special mirrors made of gold or nickel. Others have no mirrors at all. Instead, they use lead or iron slats that filter some of the X-rays into a special counting chamber filled with gas. An electronic device counts the number of times the X-rays interact with the gas.

X-ray telescopes detect objects in space that give off X-rays. The first X-ray telescope was used to study the Sun in 1963. Then, in the 1970s, an orbiting X-ray telescope on the space station Skylab took

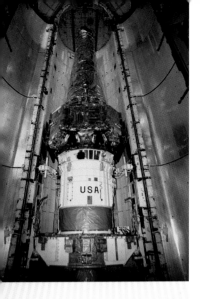

▲ *The Chandra X-ray Observatory was transported into orbit in the cargo area of the Space Shuttle* Columbia *in 1999. Scientists in Cambridge, Massachusetts, control Chandra.*

more than 35,000 pictures of the Sun. X-ray telescopes have also been used to study the hot gases in galaxies and supernovas.

The Chandra X-Ray Observatory, launched into Earth orbit in 1999, captures and records high resolution X-ray data emitted by supernovas and black holes. Chandra produces incredibly clear X-ray images. In fact, if Chandra operated in visible light, it could read a stop sign from 12 miles (19 km) away. Astronomers from the Smithsonian Astrophysical Observatory (SAO) in Cambridge, Massachusetts, control the orbiting observatory's daily activities from the Operations Control Center and Chandra X-ray Center (CXC) facilities.

Like X-rays, gamma rays must also be observed from space. These short rays have the most energy of all types of electromagnetic radiation. Gamma rays exist in the "hottest" parts of space—the areas that produce the most radioactive energy. Black holes, pulsars, exploding supernovas, and other violent events all emit gamma rays.

Gamma ray telescopes carry special detectors called **scintillators** that detect gamma rays. The gamma ray telescope, the Compton Gamma-Ray Observatory (CGRO), launched in 1991, provided astronomers with useful information on black holes and neutron stars. NASA intentionally destroyed the CGRO in 2000 at the end of a successful mission. It burned up in Earth's atmosphere during reentry.

Perhaps the most amazing aspect of these latest telescopes is the enormous leap in technology they represent: While it took nearly four centuries to advance from the invention of the first telescope to the current orbiting telescopes, it took only three decades to make some of these orbiting space telescopes about one-billion times more powerful than the original models they replaced.

*The Telescope and Microscope*

# PEERING INTO THE FUTURE

Today's space-based telescopes provide astronomers with a wide range of information about the universe. In the early twentieth century, however, few scientists dreamed of using such valuable orbiting tools.

Earth's atmosphere distorts and bends light. Using Earth-based telescopes to research objects in space is like looking at something through a glass of water—the image is indistinct and ill-defined. Astronomers can now bypass atmospheric effects by putting their instruments directly into orbit to obtain the clearest possible images.

## Telescopes in Space

The first person to suggest the idea of creating an observatory in outer space was astronomer Lyman

▼ *The Spitzer Space Telescope's infrared array camera captured this infrared image of a stellar formation. Named after Dr. Lyman Spitzer Jr., the scientist who proposed putting telescopes in space, the Spitzer telescope's infrared detectors capture cosmic features never seen before.*

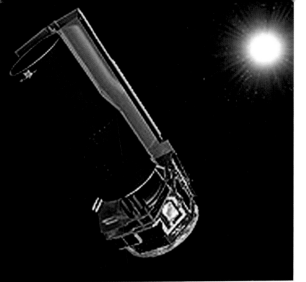

Spitzer Jr. (1914–1997). Spitzer realized that, with no atmosphere to cloud his view, he would get a clearer, sharper image of stars, planets, and other celestial bodies. In 1946, long before any satellites were launched into space, he proposed placing a telescope into space.

In 1958, the U.S. government founded the National Aeronautics and Space Administration (NASA). The organization's mission was to study flight and expand human knowledge of space. In 1972, NASA launched the *Copernicus* satellite—which Spitzer had helped design—into space. Also known as an orbiting astronomical observatory, *Copernicus* featured an ultraviolet telescope.

▲ *The Spitzer Space Telescope, shown in this artist's conception, "sees" through obscuring space dust to capture images of distant stars and other objects in the universe. The infrared telescope must remain extremely cold for proper operation. Its solar shield must always point toward the Sun.*

## The Hubble Space Telescope

In the 1970s, the United States and Europe began working together to make Spitzer's dream a reality. In 1977, NASA and the European Space Agency (ESA) started constructing the Hubble Space Telescope (HST). On April 25, 1990, the U.S. space shuttle *Discovery* placed the HST into orbit about 375 miles (603 km) above Earth's surface. Scientists and technicians monitor the movements of the HST's **gyroscopes** from Earth. Gyroscopes aboard the HST keep it pointed at its target. Astronomers use radio signals to tell the HST what to look at next.

The HST's two spectrographs, for example, separate different types of electomagnetic radiation. The telescope is also equipped with cameras that take pictures and transmit these images to Earth. The

*The Telescope and Microscope*

entire telescope is powered by two giant solar panels that convert the Sun's energy into electricity.

The quality and variety of the HST's images surpassed the wildest expectations of astronomers around the world. HST milestones include:

- The first visual evidence of black holes
- The first images of the surface of Pluto and the first clear pictures of the surface of Mars
- Images that reveal the nature of quasars—objects larger than a star but smaller than a galaxy
- Pictures of the birth and death of stars
- Images of the comet Shoemaker-Levy 9 crashing into Jupiter in 1994

Astronomers hope to use data from the HST to help them understand the size of the universe and determine its age. They also hope the HST will help them learn answers to many intergalactic mysteries and chart how the universe is evolving.

The HST was designed to work for fifteen years. Since 1990, astronauts have periodically performed maintenance operations on the HST to keep it working properly. In 1993, for example, astronauts fixed a defective mirror, allowing the telescope to capture crisper, clearer images of outer space. In 1997, astronauts attached new instruments and repaired the insulation that allows the HST to withstand the extreme temperatures of space.

After the explosion of the space shuttle *Columbia* in February 2003, future manned space missions, including one in 2004 to service the HST, were canceled. NASA is considering using ground-controlled robots to service and maintain the valuable observatory. Although the space

▼ *In 1990, the space shuttle* Discovery *'s robotic arm captured the Hubble Space Telescope for an orbiting service mission at about 380 miles (611 km) above Earth,.*

- The Hubble Space Telescope orbits the Earth every ninety-five minutes.

- Hubble is named for astronomer Edwin Hubble (1889–1953), who is best known for his work in the 1920s on the size and expansion of the universe.

- The explosion of the space shuttle *Challenger* in January 1986 delayed the HST's launch by four years. The HST was finally launched by the space shuttle *Discovery* in 1990.

- After its mirror was fixed in 1993, the HST captured some incredible images, including the famous pillars of the Eagle Nebula—a stellar nursery.

- Images and data from the HST are transmitted first to a lab at White Sands, New Mexico, and then beamed to another space satellite—which then sends the data to NASA's Goddard Space Flight Center lab in Greenbelt, Maryland.

- The HST is about the size of a school bus.

agency has a $16 billion budget for 2005, it is not certain how much of that money will go toward repairing the HST. NASA projects depend on funding from Congress.

## The Future of Space Telescopes

NASA plans to someday replace the HST with an advanced telescope called the James Webb Space Telescope (JWST). The JWST will have a larger mirror and more powerful infrared equipment than the HST. It will also weigh less than the HST, thanks to advances in technology and materials.

NASA plans to orbit the JWST about 1 million miles (1.6 million km) from the Earth, much farther away than the HST. Astronomers hope that the powerful new scope will "see" to the edges of the universe and capture images of the oldest stars and galaxies, which will provide valuable information on the birth and shape of the universe. The JWST may be ready for launching in 2011.

## Telescopes of the Future

Advances in optical technology have made optical, Earth-based telescopes more effective. One such advance is called adaptive optics, a once top-secret technology developed by the U.S. government.

Adaptive optic (AO) technology compensates for the distorting effects of the Earth's atmosphere by automatically modifying the shape of a telescope's mirrors. Telescopes using AO can achieve resolutions and produce images that rival those of orbiting telescopes. The Keck Observatory in Hawaii and the Hale Telescope in Calfornia use AO technology.

Who knows what further technological advances await future telescopes?

*The Telescope and Microscope*

# LOOKING AT TINY LIFE

While astronomers were finding ways to peer into outer space, other scientists were more concerned with taking a closer look at life on Earth.

The simple microscope is any instrument with a single lens that makes objects look larger. Centuries ago, people used glass and lenses to help them see more clearly. The very best magnifying glasses, only magnified an object only to about twenty times its normal size. No one thought about using two lenses to increase the viewing power of such a device until the late 1500s.

## From Eyeglasses to Microscopes

Like telescopes, microscopes had their start with eyeglass makers. Dutch eyeglass maker Zacharias Janssen (1580–1638) is often given credit for being the first person to build an early version of a **compound microscope** in 1590 or 1595. A compound microscope uses two or more lenses. Janssen's microscope was a simple device, made up of a lens at each end of a tube.

Galileo also contributed to the development of the microscope. In 1609, he created a device he called the *occhiolino*. The instrument used two lenses, one convex and one concave, to magnify objects. Although he would most often use his

▼ *This early example of a basic compound microscope has three objective lenses of varying magnification.*

## Lynxes and Microscopes

Johannes Faber (1574–1629) coined the word *microscope*. Faber created the word from the Greek root words *mikros*, meaning "small," and *skopein*, meaning "to look at." Like Galileo, Faber was a member of the Academia Lincei, or Academy of the Lynxes. The group, based in Rome, was a society of scholars and scientists. It is believed to be one of the world's first scientific associations. Society members named themselves for the lynx, a wildcat found in Eurasia and North America. At this time, people thought that lynxes had the ability to see in the dark. The members of the society believed that they too were doing work that would allow others to see through the darkness of ignorance.

Faber used the term *microscope* in a 1625 letter describing Galileo's invention for seeing tiny objects. The same year, academy members carefully examined a bee with the new device and published illustrations of it, which were some of the earliest pictures of an object as seen through a microscope.

invention to examine the sky, one of the first objects Galileo studied was a fly.

Ten years after the invention of Galileo's magnifying device, an English scientist named Cornelis Drebbel (1572–1633) used two convex lenses to make a compound microscope. By the 1620s, Drebbel had built a number of these magnifying machines. In 1622, one of his inventions was presented to Marie de Medici, the queen of France.

Drebbel's early invention was very basic. It consisted of a three-piece brass tube that could be extended as needed. The tube was attached to a small disk with three legs. A stage (platform) for the specimens was placed in the middle of the disk, directly below the tube. Scientists could change the size of the image by pulling or pushing the tube, making it different lengths.

*The Telescope and Microscope*

Scientists realized how important the microscope could be to increasing knowledge about the world. Several problems, however, would first have to be overcome. One of the largest obstacles was the quality of the lenses that were needed. At this time, glass grinding was difficult and time-consuming. Lenses were often quite flawed. Many, for example, contained air bubbles, which distorted the images. Until glass grinding techniques improved, microscopes were only as good as the best hand lenses.

## Robert Hooke and Micrographia

In 1665, one of the first books about the microscope and its capabilities was published. The book, called *Micrographia*, was written by Robert Hooke (1635–1703), a well-known English scientist and architect who had become fascinated by the microscope's potential. *Micrographia* included detailed images of magnified objects that Hooke drew himself. He created pictures of fleas, flies, silk, eels, burned vegetables, and much more.

One of Hooke's important observations and descriptions was of cork bark. Hooke decided that, under his microscope, the tiny particles that made up the bark looked like the cells that monks lived in. Today, Hooke's word *cell* is still used to describe the basic unit of all living matter.

Hooke, like other scientists in the late 1600s, tried to improve the compound microscope. One of his advances included a special illuminating system to light a specimen being viewed. The most powerful instrument he ever worked with, however, magnified objects only thirty times. Although this is weak by today's standards, Hooke's devices were the most powerful of his time.

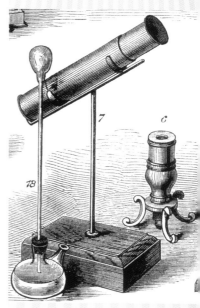

▼ *An archival drawing illustrates Galileo's thermoscope, an instrument that measured changes in temperature (left); Galileo's microscope (middle); and Zacharias Janssen's compound microscope (right).*

# Seeing "Little Animals"

In 1674, Dutchman Antonie van Leeuwenhoek (1632–1723) began using simple microscopes in his scientific experiments. Although many people had tried to improve the microscope by adding lenses, Leeuwenhoek found that using only one lens actually improved the clarity of the image.

Leeuwenhoek came up with the idea for the simple microscope while working as a linen merchant. In this job, he used a magnifying glass to count the threads in cloth. Leeuwenhoek quickly became fascinated with the idea of building a machine that could magnify tiny objects. He taught himself how to grind glass and began to make his own curved lenses. It was the only way he could ensure getting a high-quality lens.

Although crude, Leeuwenhoek's microscopes were much more accurate than previous instruments. One of his microscopes made tiny objects appear 266 times larger than normal. Because of his effective new instruments, Leeuwenhoek is often called the "father of the microscope."

Leeuwenhoek used his simple microscopes to examine drops of water and blood. He was the first person to see protozoa and **bacteria**, tiny single-celled organisms that are invisible to the human eye. When writing about his findings, Leeuwenhoek called the bacteria *animalcules*, or "little animals."

Leeuwenhoek later went on to study the life cycles of such animals as lice, fleas, and mites. He also examined animal fluids under his microscope. Leeuwenhoek's research led to a better understanding of animal and human life. His experiments also advanced the study of plant biology.

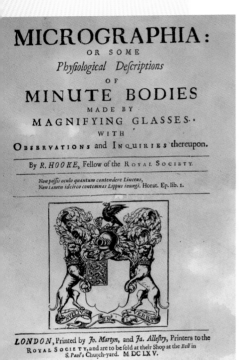

▲ Robert Hooke's book, Micrographia, contained the first illustration of cells and was a landmark in the early days of the field of microscopy.

# From Simple Back to Compound

Despite the limited capabilities of microscopes in the 1600s, scientists made some earth-shattering discoveries with these instruments. Microscope milestones during this early "golden age" of microscope research include the work of three scientists: Marcello Malpighi (1628–1694), Nehemiah Grew (1641–1712), and Jan Swammerdam (1637–1680).

Between 1661 and 1666, Italian scientist Malpighi studied the anatomy and functions of such organs as the lung, tongue, skin, brain, liver, and kidney. He also described the development of a chick within its egg. In the 1670s and 1680s, Grew, an English botanist, published a number of important works on plant biology, including *The Anatomy of Plants*. Finally, Swammerdam was probably the first person to see red blood cells through a microscope. The Dutch scientist also studied insects extensively.

During the 1700s, people interested in microscopes continued to make important changes that improved the devices. Many of these changes were in the design of the microscope tube's mount and support system.

One of the most significant changes was made by John Cuff (1708–1792), an English eyeglass and microscope maker, in the mid-1700s. Around 1744, Cuff introduced the first "user-friendly" microscope.

## Magnify This!

The power of a microscope is shown as a number and the letter *x* (for times). For example, if a microscope magnifies an object 10 times its normal size, it provides a magnification of 10x. Simple microscopes can magnify up to about 100x. Compound microscopes can magnify up to about 1,000x. Some modern microscopes, such as field-ion microscopes, can magnify up to 1,000,000x!

This new microscope allowed scientists to focus on the specimen they were examining more easily and accurately. Cuff's design also allowed scientists to move and adjust the specimen more easily.

In the beginning of the 1800s, advancements in glassmaking techniques finally led to the creation of more effective and powerful compound microscopes. By the mid-1800s, some German and American companies were manufacturing microscopes.

The microscope quickly proved a revolutionary tool for scientists. They could study the causes of disease and sickness and learn more about atoms, the basic building blocks of life, using microscopes. They could also explore the structures of metals and many other substances.

In 1831, for example, Scottish physician Robert Brown (1773–1858) used a microscope to discover a plant cell nucleus. Later observations of cells by other scientists led to the development of cell theory, the idea that all life is based on cells.

*▲ Marcello Malpighi, an Italian anatomist, published the book Anatome Plantarum, an early study of plant structure, animal development, and the anatomy and functions of organs.*

## Steps toward Better Health Care

In the 1800s, a few dedicated doctors used their study of microscopic organisms to bring about important changes in medical care. Even after scientists began studying harmful bacteria, viruses, and fungi under the microscope, some doctors refused to believe that these invisible organisms caused disease.

In the early 1860s, a Hungarian doctor named Ignaz Phillipp Semmelweis (1818–1865) was mocked by fellow physicians for his assertion that they could easily reduce the death rate at hospitals by washing their hands. Semmelweis had developed his theory while working in the maternity ward of an Austrian hospital. At that time, between 10 and 15 percent of all new mothers died after giving birth in the hospital. Semmelweis came to the conclusion that the cause of death was an infectious disease, spread by doctors who examined women after handling dead bodies.

Unfortunately, Semmelweis did not look for hard evidence for his theory by examining fluids from the dead bodies under a microscope. Many experts, therefore, refused to accept his ideas. Despite the public ridicule, Semmelweis persisted in promoting sanitary, sterile practices in hospitals. Thanks to his efforts, many hospitals eventually adopted these procedures. As a result, hospital death rates, especially in maternity wards, dropped drastically.

Later, Joseph Lister (1827–1912) expanded on Semmelweis's work. He began the practice of boiling surgical instruments to kill bacteria. In 1865, Lister also started using antiseptics—germ-killing chemicals—during surgery. Death rates as a result of post-surgical infections dropped from 50 percent to almost none.

Also in the 1860s, a French scientist named Louis Pasteur (1822–1895) performed some of the most important early studies on bacteria and other microorganisms. Pasteur used a microscope to study bacteria in wine. He showed that heating the wine killed the bacteria, a process that came to be known as pasteurization. This process is still used today to preserve foods, especially milk. Before pasteurization, people could become very ill from ingesting disease-causing bacteria present in raw milk.

## Fast Fact

Louis Pasteur made great contributions to the field of microbiology. In addition to pasteurization, he discovered that weaker forms of viruses could be used to immunize people and animals against them. Pasteur also discovered that the highly infectious rabies virus was too small to see under a microscope.

# 6 TYPES OF MICROSCOPES

▶ *All compound microscopes have several parts in common. The lens at the top of the tube is called the eyepiece or ocular. The eyepiece magnifies the image produced by the objective, the lens or lenses at the opposite end of the tube.*

*The specimen is placed on the stage, a flat surface attached to the body of the microscope. The base usually contains a light source or a mirror to reflect light through the condenser lens situated just below the stage. The condenser lens directs the light onto the specimen.*

*The objective provides the resolution (clarity) and magnifying power needed to produce an image. A rotating nosepiece holds the lenses for compound microscopes with more than one objective lens.*

S imple and compound microscopes are known as optical, or light, microscopes: They use light and lenses to magnify small objects. The lenses of the microscope refract, or bend, light, directing the light rays onto the object being viewed.

Most simple microscopes are hand-held devices with a single lens or set of lenses. One type of simple microscope is the loupe, a small eyepiece used by photographers, artists, jewelers, and watchmakers. Another type of simple microscope is the hand lens, also known as a magnifying glass. The most powerful simple microscopes have a magnification power of about 25x.

## Basic Parts of the Compound Microscope

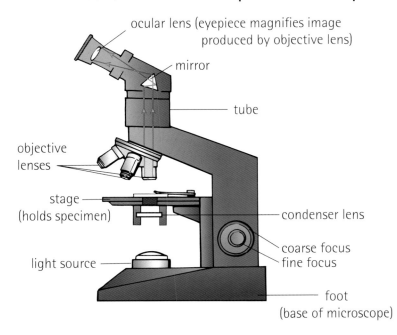

ocular lens (eyepiece magnifies image produced by objective lens)

mirror

tube

objective lenses

stage (holds specimen)

condenser lens

coarse focus
fine focus

light source

foot (base of microscope)

# The Science of Microtomy

Scientists soon learned that to successfully view an object under a microscope, they needed to prepare it in some way. The processes involved in this task led to the technical side of tissue preparation, or the science of microtomy. Modern laboratory technicians now use a number of techniques called smears, squashes, whole mounts, and thin sectioning to prepare samples for examination under a light microscope. Technicians use special dyes to highlight different parts of the tissues or cells they wish to study.

German scientist Paul Ehrlich (1854–1915) developed some specialized dyes for tissues. In the early 1900s, Ehrlich became convinced that some dyes and chemicals might be used to treat and cure disease. Today, this branch of medical science is known as chemotherapy. Ehrlich's studies in the field led to greater scientific knowledge of diphtheria, tuberculosis, cancer, and other diseases. Ehrlich is credited with pioneering the science of hematology, the study of blood, by creating a special stain used to prepare blood cells for viewing.

## Paul Ehrlich

As a child, Paul Ehrlich became infected by the deadly disease tuberculosis, which may have prompted his lifelong interest in the treatment of disease. He was the first scientist to develop a chemical approach to treating disease. Ehrlich envisioned "magic bullets," chemical compounds that would enter the body and attack specific disease-causing organisms. His early work concentrating on the use of chemical dyes to stain tissue samples revealed that certain dyes reacted to different samples in particular ways. With this knowledge, Ehrlich concentrated on which dyes seemed to attack bacterial toxins but left healthy cells intact. Ehrlich received the Nobel Prize in medicine in 1908.

Most basic compound microscopes have three objective lenses: 4x, 10x, and 40x. If a microscope has a 10x ocular lens, the total magnification power is 40x, 100x, and 400x, respectively.

▼ *Today, students use microscopes in class to learn about cell structure. Daniel Rotenbury, a seventh-grader at Kingman Junior High School in Kingman, Arizona, sets onion cells in place so he can study them and reproduce their design in a drawing.*

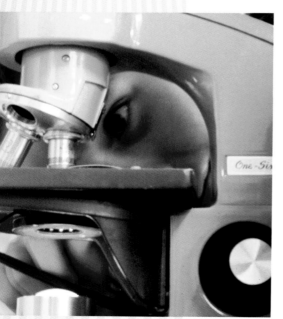

# The Compound Microscope Evolves

In the twentieth century, scientists continued to make improvements in compound microscopes. Today, scientists use a varitey of specialized compound microscopes and techniques for viewing specimens. These different tools allow scientists to study a wide variety of materials and objects. They can choose the best microscope for the specimen they are studying.

One specialized compound microscope is the ultramicroscope, which was invented in 1903. The ultramicroscope is used to examine **colloidal solutions**. A colloid is a material made of tiny particles of one substance that are spread evenly throughout another substance. Colloidal particles are too tiny to be seen with a regular optical microscope, so scientists suspend the colloidal particles in a liquid and light the solution from the side. Using the ultramicroscope, they can see particles that are as small as thirty-nine billionths of an inch (0.0009906 microns).

The phase-contrast microscope, developed in the 1930s, is used to study unstained living cells. It makes some parts of the cell seem lighter and some seem darker. Another special type of compound microscope is the television microscope. This type of instrument uses ultraviolet light and a special camera to create colorized images of objects. The images can be viewed on a television screen connected to the microscope.

In the early 1900s, scientists developed dark-field microscopy. This technique allows scientists to see images that are invisible with normal lighting. With dark-field microscopy, a special **condenser lens** creates a bright image of the specimen on a dark background.

# MICROSCOPES TODAY

The twentieth century saw the invention of some amazing new microscopes. These instruments gave scientists a look at objects that had once been hidden, even from the most powerful compound microscopes available.

## Electron Microscopes

One of the most exciting inventions of the 1930s was the electron microscope. The electron microscope (EM) does not use optical lenses and light to magnify an image. Instead, magnetic lenses focus a beam of **electrons** on the specimen. Electrons are tiny particles with a negative electrical charge. All atoms have at least one electron. The EM's lenses create a magnetic field that focuses the electrons onto the object, producing an image on a fluorescent screen.

Because electrons have shorter wavelengths than visible light rays, electron microscopes provide greater magnification than optical microscopes. This gives scientists a detailed look at specimens. This type of microscope is useful for looking at cell structure and the atoms that make up metals and other substances.

▼ *University of Florida engineering professor Rajiv Singh uses an electron microscope with a maximum resolution 400,000 times smaller than the diameter of a human hair. Researchers use this microscope, one of the most powerful in the world, to learn how to make better computer chips and more effective drugs.*

The electron microscope has some limitations. Specimens must be placed in a vacuum (a space without any air) before being viewed. As a result, electron microscopes cannot be used to examine live objects. In addition, the electron beam can damage a specimen, so scientists must take special care when preparing an object for examination.

There are several types of electron microscopes. Two of the most important are the transmission electron microscope and the scanning electron microscope.

The transmission electron microscope (TEM) was developed in 1931 by German scientist Ernst Ruska (1906–1988). This type of microscope is used to create a fluorescent image of very thin specimen slices. Electrons pass through the object and are focused onto a fluorescent screen. Scientists can use a camera inside a TEM to take photographs of the images they see. This type of device is most often used to study the components of cells.

In 1966, the scanning electron microscope (SEM) was introduced. The SEM is even more powerful than the transmission electron microscope. It uses a focused beam of electrons that produces an image by scanning a specimen section by section. An enlarged image of the specimen's surface is then transmitted to a television screen.

## Scanning Probe Microscopes

Another type of microscope is the scanning probe microscope. The scanning probe microscope uses a probe, or sharp point, to explore the surface of an object. This type of microscope creates three-dimensional pictures of the tiny object. It is an important research tool for physicists, chemists, and engineers. Physicists and other scientists use these microscopes to examine single atoms that are not visible with other types of microscopes. Engineers use them to study the surface structure of various metals. They can examine the metals for surface flaws and weaknesses. This information is important for building strong, long-lasting buildings, bridges, and ships.

There are several types of scanning probe microscopes. One type, the scanning tunneling microscope (STM), was invented in 1981 by West German scientist Gerd Binnig (b. 1947) and Swiss scientist Heinrich Rohrer (b. 1933). The STM uses a metal probe to scan the specimen with a field of electrons. The electrons move between the probe and the surface of the specimen, responding to any changes in texture. The information captured by the scan is translated into a three-dimensional map of the object's surface.

The STM can only be used to study objects that conduct electricity. That's because the probe creates an electrical current between it and the object. The microscope is so powerful that it can provide clear, detailed images of single atoms. It is most often used to examine the surfaces of metals. Research conducted with the STM has led to the development of superstrong artificial materials used in the making of CD players, computers, and wireless telephones.

Another type of scanning probe microscope is the atomic force microscope (AFM). The probe of the AFM actually comes in gentle contact with the specimen. The probe moves up and down over the object, mapping its surface. Unlike the STM, the AFM can be used to examine materials that do not conduct electricity, such as some chemicals, cells, molecules, and magnetic disks. Computer scientists are using the AFM to increase the amount of data that today's computers can hold.

▲ A Hewlett Packard Company researcher, R. Stanley Williams, works on a scanning tunneling microscope (STM), at the company's headquarters in Palo Alto, California. Capable of seeing individual atoms, the STM is an essential tool in the field of nanotechnology—the science and technology of building super-miniaturized machines from single atoms and molecules.

## Fast Fact

In 1986, Binnig and Rohrer were awarded the Nobel Prize in physics for the scanning tunneling microscope.

Other types of scanning probe microscopes react to an object's temperature, ability to reflect light, and chemical changes.

## The Ion Microscope

The ion microscope is especially useful in the study of metals. This microscope is one of the most powerful magnifying tools available to scientists. Instead of electrons, the ion microscope uses positive ions to magnify an object. An ion is an atom that has a negative or positive charge as a result of having lost or gained one or more electrons.

The ion microscope uses a supersharp needle that is made of the metal being studied. An electrical field between the needle and a screen causes atoms from the needle's tip to strike the screen and glow. The device creates a magnified image of the arrangement of atoms in the metal.

The ion microscope was created in 1951 by German scientist Erwin W. Muller (1911–1977). Three years later, he developed an even more specialized version of his microscope. Like the STM, the new microscope, called the atom-probe field-ion microscope, can examine a single atom. It is powerful enough to magnify an object up to one million times! The microscope is used to examine metals.

Today, microscopes continue to be used to study the atomic structure of different metals. Microscopes are also used in the computer field to allow technicians to examine the tiniest computer chips.

## Acoustic Microscopes and Other Advances

Acoustic microscopes enable researchers to use sounds to create crisp, clear pictures of an object.

*The Telescope and Microscope*

## The Art of Photomicrography

Photomicrography is the science of taking pictures of microscope images. To take a photo of a magnified object, photographers place a camera over the microscope's eyepiece. In recent years, advances in camera technology have elevated photomicrography to a unique form of art. Photographers have gone from using cameras with film to electronic and digital media. Instead of a long, intensive development process, they can now download images onto a computer and work from there, editing the image to suit their artistic vision.

Acoustic microscopy is used by people researching design and structural flaws deep inside equipment or materials made of metal, ceramics, and many other substances. The acoustic microscope can also create an image of the material's surface.

The digital microscope is another innovation. It plugs into a computer, takes a digital picture of a specimen, and then transfers the image to the computer's monitor. Some digital microscopes have no eyepieces, although others do. Like the television microscope, the digital microscope allows more than one person to view a specimen at one time. It can capture stunning color images of magnified objects.

One of the most recent advances in microscopy is the virtual microscope. People with Internet access can visit Web sites and view online images of various specimens as seen through different types of microscopes. Some sites allow users to the change focus, magnification, and brightness of the image.

Today, telescope and microscope technology continues to advance. Computers have revolutionized the way both instruments are used. Each decade, scientists discover new objects in space and reach new milestones in medicine and microbiology. As a result, people's understanding of the world around them continues to expand.

# TIME LINE

| | |
|---|---|
| **1609** | Galileo Galilei creates a refracting telescope to view the skies. |
| **1619** | Cornelis Drebbel builds the first compound microscope. |
| **1668** | Sir Isaac Newton invents the first working reflecting telescope. |
| **1672** | Cassegrain invents an improved reflecting telescope. |
| **c. 1673** | Polish astronomer Johannes Hevelius builds a large refracting telescope that measures 150 feet (46 m) long. |
| **c. 1744** | John Cuff introduces the first easy-to-use microscope. |
| **1800** | Sir William Herschel discovers infrared radiation. |
| **1801** | Johann Wilhelm Ritter discovers ultraviolet radiation. |
| **1897** | The world's largest refracting telescope goes into operation at the Yerkes Observatory in Williams Bay, Wisconsin. |
| **1903** | The ultramicroscope is invented. |
| **1917** | Scientists construct the Hooker Telescope at Mount Wilson Observatory. |
| **1919–1924** | Edwin Hubble uses the Hooker Telescope to prove the existence of galaxies other than the Milky Way. |
| **1930** | Bernhard Schmidt invents the catadioptric telescope, which combines elements of the refracting and reflecting scopes. |
| **1931** | The first electron microscope is built by Ernst Ruska. |
| **1932** | Karl Guthe Jansky invents one of the first radio telescopes. |
| **1948** | A telescope with a 200-inch mirror is built on Palomar Mountain in California. |
| **1951** | The ion microscope is invented by German scientist Erwin W. Muller. |
| **1958** | The U.S. government founds the National Aeronautics and Space Administration (NASA) to study space. |
| **1963** | The largest radio telescope in the world is built near Arecibo, Puerto Rico. The first X-ray telescope is used to study the Sun. |
| **1978** | The International Ultraviolet Explorer telescope is launched into space, providing scientists with information about black holes, solar winds, and new galaxies. |
| **1981** | The scanning tunneling microscope is invented. |
| **1990** | The Hubble Space Telescope is placed into orbit above Earth. |
| **1993** | Keck Observatory in Hawaii goes into operation. |
| **2000** | Virtual microscope Web sites become available. |

# GLOSSARY

**aperture:** the diameter of a telescope's objective lens

**astrolabe:** a metal disk on a round frame, used to measure the altitude, or height, of stars and planets above the horizon

**bacteria:** microscopic, single-celled organisms

**binocular microscope:** a microscope that has two eyepieces

**charge-coupled device (CCD):** an electronic sensor that takes digital pictures of the sky

**colloidal solutions:** solutions made up of tiny particles of one substance that are spread evenly throughout another substance

**compound microscope:** a microscope that uses two or more lenses

**concave:** curving inward

**condenser lens:** the lens on a microscope that directs light onto the specimen being viewed

**constellations:** groupings of stars as seen from Earth

**convex:** curved outward

**corrector lens:** a telescope lens specially designed to bend light rays and correct the blurriness of a telescope's image

**electrons:** tiny particles with a negative electrical charge

**extreme ultraviolet rays:** very short ultraviolet wavelengths

**gyroscopes:** tools that move a telescope and keep it pointed at its target

**infrared array detector:** a device on an infrared telescope that takes the place of the CCD on a regular reflecting telescope

**infrared radiation:** light rays with a longer wavelength than visible light rays

**monocular microscope:** a microscope that has just one eyepiece

**optical telescopes:** telescopes that work with visible light rays

**quadrant:** an instrument, shaped like a quarter of a circle, used to measure the altitude, or height, of a star or planet

**reflecting telescope:** a telescope that works by gathering, focusing, and magnifying light rays emitted by an object

**refracting telescope:** a telescope that works by focusing light rays and directing them to an eyepiece

**scintillators:** detectors on gamma ray telescopes that locate gamma rays

**wavelength:** the distance between the peak of one wave of light and the peak of the next wave

# FOR MORE INFORMATION

## Books

Kramer, Stephen. *Hidden Worlds: Looking through a Scientist's Microscope.* Boston: Houghton Mifflin, 2001.

Morris, Neil. *Astronomers.* North Mankato, Illinois: Chrysalis Education, 2003.

Ride, Sally. *Exploring Our Universe.* New York: Crown, 2003.

Salamony, Sandra, ed. *Sky and Telescope's Beautiful Universe: The Most Awesome and Inspiring Images of the Heavens.* Cambridge, Massachusetts: Sky Publishing, 2004.

Woog, Adam. *The Microscope: Great Medical Discoveries.* San Diego: Lucent, 2003.

## Videos and DVDs

Filippenko, Alex. *Understanding the Universe: An Introduction to Astronomy.* Springfield, Virginia: Teaching Company, 2001.

*The Incredible World of the Microscope.* Raleigh, North Carolina: Rainbow Educational Media, 2001.

Pomasanoff, Alex. *The Invisible World.* Burbank, California: National Geographic Society, 1994.

*Sir Isaac Newton: The Gravity of Genius.* New York: A&E Home Video, 2004.

*Stargaze: Hubble's View of the Universe.* Gambrills, Maryland: AlphaDVD, 2000.

## Web Sites

*http://antwrp.gsfc.nasa.gov/apod/* View a new satellite image each day, courtesy of NASA.

*http://micro.magnet.fsu.edu/index.html* Molecular Expressions Web site with a Museum of Microscopy, images of objects as seen through optical microscopes, and related links.

*http://xmm.vilspa.esa.es/external/xmm_science/gallery/public/index.php* Photos from the XMM-Newton Observatory.

*www.microscopy-uk.org.uk/micropolitan/* The Micropolitan Museum of Microscopic Art Forms includes images of creatures such as water fleas, snails, flatworms, and much more.

*www.pbrc.hawaii.edu/bemf/microangela/* Bugs, bacteria, and body parts like you've never seen them before: images from electron microscopes at the University of Hawaii.

# INDEX

acoustic microscopes
42–43
adaptive optics 28
AFM (atomic force
microscope) 41
antiseptic 35
apertures 17
Arecibo Radio
Telescope 19
astronomy
early instruments for
6–8
Galileo's telescope
and 9, 10
reflecting telescope
for 12
space telescopes
25–28
telescope improve-
ments 13–14
twentieth-century tel-
escopes 14–16
types of telescopes
for 17–24
atomic force micro-
scopes (AFM) 41
atom-probe field-ion
microscopes 42
atoms 39, 40–41, 42

Bacon, Roger 6
bacteria 32, 34–35
Binnig, Gerd 41
binocular
microscopes 37
binoculars 17
black holes 23, 24, 27
Brown, Robert 34
Burnell, Jocelyn Bell 20

Cassegrain, N. 12–13
catadioptric
telescopes 14
cathode 40
CCD (charge-coupled
device) 18
cells 31, 32, 39, 40
cell theory 34
CGRO (Compton
Gamma-Ray
Observatory) 24
Challenger space
shuttle 28

Chandra X-Ray
Observatory 24
charge-coupled devices
(CCD) 18
chemotherapy 37
Coblentz, William
Weber 20
colloidal solutions 38
Columbia space
shuttle 27
compound microscopes
29–31, 36, 38
Compton Gamma-Ray
Observatory
(CGRO) 24
condenser lenses 38
Copernicus,
Nicolaus 10
Copernicus satellite 26
corrector lenses 14
cross staff 8
Cuff, John 33–34

dark-field
microscopy 38
della Spina,
Alexandro 6
digital microscopes 43
Discovery space shuttle
26, 27
diseases 8
dishes 18, 19
Drebbel, Cornelis 30
dyes 37

Ehrlich, Paul 37
Einstein, Albert 27
electron microscopes
39–40
European Space Agency
(ESA) 26
extreme ultraviolet
rays 22
eyeglasses 6, 29

Faber, Johannes 30

Galilei, Galileo 9–10,
29–30, 31
gamma ray telescopes
23, 24
Gershon, Levi ben
7–8

glass lenses
of catadioptric tele-
scope 14
of early microscopes
29–30, 31, 32
invention of 6
invention of tele-
scope and 9–10
microscope advance-
ments 34
Gregory, James 12
Grew, Nehemiah 33
gyroscopes 26

Hale, George Elliot 15
Hale Telescope 28
Halley's comet 18
hand lens 36
health care 34–35
hematology 37
Herschel, William
13–14, 20
Hevelius, Johannes 11
Hewlett Packard
Company 41
Hippocrates 8
Hooker, John D. 15
Hooke, Robert 31, 32
Hooker telescope 15
Hopkins Ultraviolet
Telescope (HUT)
22–23
Hubble, Edwin 15, 28
Hubble Space Telescope
26–28

infrared array
detectors 20
Infrared Astronomy
Satellite (IRAS) 21
infrared radiation
19–21
infrared telescopes
19–21, 25
International Ultraviolet
Explorer (IUE) 22
Internet 43
ion microscopes 42

James Webb Space
Telescope (JWST) 28
Jansky, Karl Guthe 19

Janssen, Zacharias
29, 31
Jupiter 10, 27

Keck Observatory
21, 22, 28
Kuiper Airborne
Observatory (KAO)
20–21

light rays
invisible/visible 20
nanometers 22
optical microscopes
and 36
reflecting telescopes
and 12
refracting telescopes
and 9, 10
light rays, invisible
infrared telescopes
for 19–21
radio telescopes for
18–19
space telescopes and
25–28
ultraviolet telescopes
21–23
X rays/gamma rays
23–24
Lippershey, Hans 9
Lister, Joseph 35
loupes 36–37
Lynx Arc megastar
clusters 22

Macrobius,
Ambrosius 4
magnification 33, 39
magnifying glasses 29
magnifying lenses 6
Maksutov-Cassegrain
telescope 14
Malpighi, Marcello
33, 34
Mars 27
merkhet 7
metals 41, 42
Michelson, Albert 15
microorganisms
34–35

microscopes
  acoustic microscopes
    42–43
  advancements 33–34
  compound; advance-
    ments 38
  compound; develop-
    ment 29–31
  digital/virtual 43
  electron microscopes
    39–40
  ion microscopes 42
  medical care changes
    34–35
  Robert Hooke
    and 31
  scanning probe
    microscopes 40–41
  simple 32
  types of 36–38
microtomy 37
mirrors
  of big telescopes 15
  of catadioptric
    telescopes 14
  of Keck
    Observatory 21
  of reflecting
    telescopes 12, 13
  of X-ray
    telescopes 23
monocular
  microscopes 37
Moon, the 9, 10
Mount Wilson
  Observatory 15
Muller, Erwin W. 42

nanometers 22
nanotechnology 41
National Aeronautics
  and Space
  Administration

(NASA) 26–28
Newton, Isaac 11–12

objective lenses 9, 17
occhiolino 29–30
ocular lenses 9
optical telescopes 17–18

pasteurization 35
Pasteur, Louis 35
phase-contrast micro-
  scope 38
photomicrography 43
Pluto 27
protozoa 32
Ptolemy 7
pulsars 19, 24

quadrants 8
quasars 27

radio telescopes 18–19
radio waves 18–19
reflecting telescope
  improvements 12–13
  as infrared
    telescopes 20
  invention of 11–12
  largest 15
  as optical
    telescopes 17
refracting-reflecting telescopes 14
refracting telescopes
  invention of 9–10
  largest 15
  as optical
    telescopes 17
Ritter, Johann
  Wilhelm 21
Rohrer, Heinrich 41
Rotenbury, Daniel 38
Ruska, Ernst 40

satellites 21, 25–28
scanning electron
  microscopes 40
scanning probe
  microscopes 40–41
scanning tunneling
  microscope
  (STM) 41
Schmidt, Bernhard 14
Schmidt-Cassegrain
  telescope 14
scientific method 5
scintillators 24
Search for
  Extraterrestrial
  Intelligence (SETI) 18
Semmelweis, Ignaz
  Phillipp 34–35
Shoemaker-Levy 9
  comet 27
sickness 8
simple microscopes
  32, 36
Singh, Rajiv 39
sounds 42–43
space telescopes
  25–28
specimens 40, 41, 43
Spitzer, Lyman, Jr.
  25–26
Spitzer Space Telescope
  25–26
starburst galaxy 21
stars 6–8, 10, 20
STM (scanning tunnel-
  ing microscope) 41
Sun 10, 24
supernovas 24
Swammerdam, Jan 33

telescopes
  catadioptric 14
  function of 5

future of 28
  improvements 12–14
  infrared 19–21
  making 16
  optical 17–18
  radio 18–19
  reflecting 11–12
  refracting 9–10
  space telescopes
    25–28
  ultraviolet 21–23
  X-ray, gamma ray
    23–24
television
  microscopes 38
thermoscopes 31
transmission electron
  microscopes 40

ultramicroscopes 38
ultraviolet telescopes
  21–23, 26
ultraviolet (UV) rays
  21–23
universe 10, 15
Uranus 13

van Leeuwenhoek,
  Antonie 32, 33
Venus 14
Very Large Array 19
virtual telescope 43

wavelengths 19–20, 23
Williams, Stanley 41

X-ray telescopes 23–24

Yerkes Observatory 15
yoke 17–18

## Author Biography

Robin Doak is a writer of fiction and nonfiction books for children, ranging from elementary to high school levels. Subjects she has written on include the human body, profiles of U.S. presidents, athletes, and American immigration. Robin is a former editor of *Weekly Reader* and, in addition to her extensive experience writing for children, has also written numerous support guides for educators. Robin holds a Bachelor of Arts degree in English from the University of Connecticut.